Investigating Unsolved Mysteries

MERMAIDS
MYTH OR REALITY?

by Lori Hile

CAPSTONE PRESS
a capstone imprint

Edge Books are published by Capstone Press,
1710 Roe Crest Drive, North Mankato, Minnesota 56003
www.capstonepub.com

Library of Congress Cataloging-in-Publication Data
Names: Hile, Lori, author.
Title: Mermaids : myth or reality? / by Lori Hile.
Description: North Mankato, Minnesota : Capstone Press, [2019] | Series:
Edge books. Investigating unsolved mysteries | Audience: Age 10. | Audience:
Grade 4 to 6. | Includes bibliographical references and index.
Identifiers: LCCN 2018005783 (print) | LCCN 2018007068 (ebook) |
ISBN 9781543535754 (eBook PDF) | ISBN 9781543535679 (library binding: alk.
paper) | ISBN 9781543535716 (paperback: alk. paper) Subjects: LCSH:
Mermaids—Juvenile literature. Classification: LCC GR910 (ebook) | LCC GR910
.H544 2019 (print) | DDC, 398.21—dc23
LC record available at https://lccn.loc.gov/2018005783

Editorial Credits
Mandy Robbins, editor; Kayla Rossow, designer; Morgan Walters,
media researcher; Gene Bentdahl, production specialist

Photo Credits
Alamy: PhotoStock-Israel, top right 13, Rik Hamilton, top 7; Getty Images: De
Agostini Picture Library, bottom right 27; iStockphoto: Yuri_Arcurs, bottom
left 7; Minden Pictures: Jeffrey Rotman, top left 21; Newscom: Album/Prisma,
middle 25, The Print Collector Heritage Images, bottom 22; Shutterstock:
AlenaLazareva, top right 9, Alex Couto, top right 17, Alex Pix, bottom right
5, Alex Tihonovs, spread 4-5, background 32, back cover, Andrea Izzotti, 1,
AOlha Rohulya, baackground 7, Art Babych, bottom right 8, Ase, background
27, Bruce Raynor, bottom right 19, Dancestrokes, top right 19, Darjus Urbanovic,
background 23, fotomika, background 25, FWStudio, (chalk texture) design
element throughout, Galina Savina, bottom right 21, I love photo, top left
23, Iakov Kalinin, background 9, Irina Alexandrovna, Cover, middle 31, Jeff
Stamer, bottom left 17, JeniFoto, background 11, KYPhua, background 21,
Lena_graphics, bottom 14, Maximum Exposure PR, background 13, Mostafa
A. Elbrolosy, bottom right 13, Olesya Baron, top right 11, Olga Bogatyrenko,
background 19, pisaphotography, background 15, Polly Dawson, spread
2-3, prapann, top right 15, SHIN-db, top 29, top 30, Svetlana Prikhnenko,
background 28, titoOnz, bottom right 10, Yulia Moiseeva, background 17

Printed and bound in the USA.   PA017

TABLE OF CONTENTS

Introduction
UNDER THE SEA. 4

Chapter 1
ENCOUNTERS WITH MERMAIDS 6

Chapter 2
USING SCIENCE TO INVESTIGATE MERMAIDS. . 14

Chapter 3
STUDYING THE EVIDENCE AND THEORIES 20

Chapter 4
CAN THE MYSTERY BE SOLVED?. 26

Summing Up the Science 28
Timeline 29
Glossary 30
Read More 31
Internet Sites 31
Index 32

Introduction

UNDER THE SEA

Throughout history, people around the world have told stories of mermaids. These strange sea creatures have the head and arms of a human. But they have the scales and tail of a fish. Mermaids are usually described as beautiful creatures. Many have long, blond locks and rosy cheeks.

Some tales about mermaids are clearly myths. But in the past, sailors and explorers have also reported mermaids as fact. What do you think? Do mermaids truly exist? Read real-life accounts of people who claim to have seen mermaids. Can science solve the mystery once and for all?

Portrait of a Mermaid

Mermaids have long been thought to possess certain characteristics, including:

- *Special talents.* It is said that some mermaids have the ability to grant wishes, tell the future, or shape shift into other bodies.
- *Beauty.* Mermaids are often pictured lying on rocks while holding a mirror or combing their long, flowing locks.
- *Enchanting singing voices.* Some people say mermaids attract sailors to rocky shores with their lovely melodies.

FACT
Not all mermaids are female. Male human sea creatures, usually called "mermen," have also been sighted and featured in stories.

CHAPTER 1
ENCOUNTERS WITH MERMAIDS

 Mermaid encounters have happened throughout the world and over hundreds of years. But do any of the encounter stories count as proof?

A Fish-Woman

In the early 1400s, a storm raged over the North Sea. The storm blew a strange, sleeping creature into Zuiderzee Bay in the Netherlands. The creature washed across the bay and into Lake Purmer, in the village of Edam.

After the storm several young women sailed across flooded fields to milk their cows. As they neared the water's edge, one of the women screamed. There lay a creature covered by a tangle of moss and seaweed. The creature had the face and upper body of a woman. But instead of legs, the creature's body curved into the tail of a fish!

The young women rescued the creature. They dressed her in clothing and fed her. They tried teaching her how to speak. But the creature could only make strange singsong sounds. Soon the fish-woman learned to spin wool into yarn. But she seldom smiled and was often seen gazing sadly toward the sea.

A present-day harbor in Edam, the Netherlands

After she died, local people gave the strange creature a proper burial. A statue of a mermaid was built next to the Purmer Gate in Edam. On it, these words were printed: "This statue was erected [built] in memory of what had been caught in Lake Purmer in the year 1403."

FACT

Mermaids have also been called sirens. A siren is a sea-dwelling creature from ancient Greek **mythology**. Sirens were said to lure sailors to their deaths with haunting songs.

mythology—old or ancient stories told again and again that help connect people with their past

Blue-Haired Mermaid?

In 1610 Captain Richard Whitbourne stood on the shore of St. John's Bay in Newfoundland, Canada. He saw something swimming swiftly toward him. It had a round face with delicate features. Long, blue hair streamed past a cream-colored neck. Its shoulders and back were as smooth as those of a human. But the creature's lower body was long and pointed, like an arrow.

The figure dove into the waves and swam toward Whitbourne's ship. Crew members aboard the ship watched as the creature wriggled toward them. Then it propped its hands on the side of the boat. The creature prepared to lunge at them. One of the men struck it on the head with an oar. The blow sent the sea creature spiraling back into the chilly Atlantic waters. Whitbourne later wrote, "This, I suppose, was a mermaid."

St. John's Bay, Newfoundland, Canada

Caribbean Creature

In 1614 English captain John Smith noticed a lady swimming near the Caribbean coast. He found her large eyes, short nose, long ears, and green hair attractive. He even experienced pangs of love. He leaned down from his ship to talk with the uncommon woman. Smith was shocked by what he saw. From the waist down, the woman was fish!

A Modern Mermaid?

In 1967 a ferryboat was traveling near Vancouver Island, in Canada. The ferry entered Active Pass, a narrow passage between islands. Several passengers on board noticed a creature sitting on some rocks. As they moved closer, they got a better look at it. It had long, blond hair and the lower body of a porpoise! The creature was calmly munching on a piece of salmon. A plane buzzed overhead around the same time, and a passenger snapped a picture of the creature. A local newspaper published the photo, along with news of the sighting.

It turned out the passengers had actually seen a mermaid—just not a real one. A woman had dressed up like a mermaid to promote a fishing event.

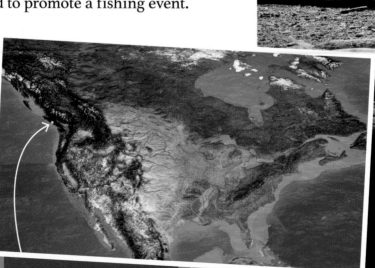

Vancouver Island, Canada

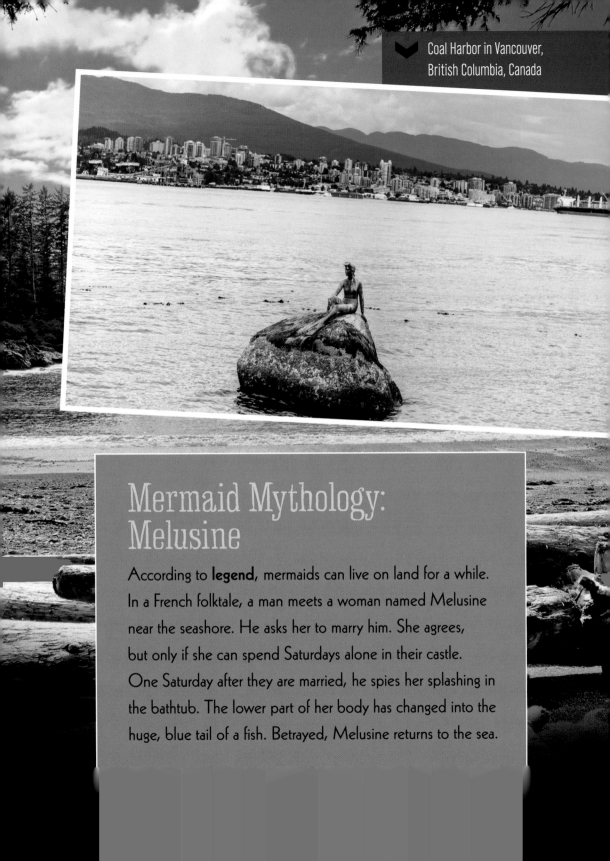

Mermaid Mythology: Melusine

According to **legend**, mermaids can live on land for a while.
In a French folktale, a man meets a woman named Melusine
near the seashore. He asks her to marry him. She agrees,
but only if she can spend Saturdays alone in their castle.
One Saturday after they are married, he spies her splashing in
the bathtub. The lower part of her body has changed into the
huge, blue tail of a fish. Betrayed, Melusine returns to the sea.

A Million Dollar Mermaid

Shlomo Cohen was walking along a beach with friends near Kiryat Yam, Israel, in 2009. He saw a woman sprawled on the sand at a strange angle. At first, Cohen thought she was just another sunbather. But as he approached the woman, she leapt into the water. Cohen could see that she had a tail like a dolphin!

Soon the town was flooded with sightings of the unusual fish-woman. Around sunset the half-girl, half-fish would appear. She performed a series of acrobatic tricks before vanishing into the waves. News of the mermaid drew crowds of people with cameras to the beach. The town even offered $1 million to anyone who could prove the mermaid's existence.

A Mermaid Mirage

In 1951 Cleo Rosin was at the Zambezi River in Zimbabwe. The 16-year-old spied an island that she'd never seen before. But even more amazing was what she saw sitting at the island's edge. It was a beautiful woman with long, black hair, completely naked. The lower part of the woman's body curved into a fish tail. Rosin looked away for a moment. When she looked again, the woman vanished. Had Rosin really seen a mermaid? Or were her eyes playing tricks on her?

A statue sits at Haifa Bay in Israel where witnesses claimed to see a mermaid in 2009.

A boy sits at the edge of the Zambezi River.

CHAPTER 2
USING SCIENCE TO INVESTIGATE MERMAIDS

 Almost every culture and country has stories about mermaids. As the study of science spread in the 1700s, educated people started to question the idea of mermaids. But that did not stop other people from spotting them. Could mermaids exist? Or is there another explanation?

The Scientific Method

Can the mystery of mermaids ever be solved? Look at the evidence presented in the stories. Can it be tested with the scientific method? Good investigators follow the scientific method when they need to establish and test a theory. The scientific method has a few basic steps:

1. Ask questions.
2. Do background research.
3. Put together an idea, called a **hypothesis**.
4. Test your hypothesis with an experiment.
5. Study the results of your experiment. What did you learn?
6. Draw conclusions. Based on your results, is your idea true? Is it partially true? Or is it completely untrue?
7. Tell people about your results.

hypothesis—a prediction that can be tested about how a scientific investigation or experiment will turn out

Mistaken for Mermaids

Many scientists have a way to explain mermaid sightings. They believe that people who think they've seen mermaids actually saw other creatures. Creatures that we already know exist could be mistaken for mermaids. Can you think of any such creatures?

Manatees

Is it possible that manatees are sometimes mistaken for mermaids? At first, manatees may seem like an unlikely candidate. Instead of slender, graceful figures, manatees have large, cucumber-shaped bodies. They weigh eight times more than the average human. At 13 feet (4 meters), they are also more than twice as long. Their skin is rough and gray. Instead of arms, they have rounded flippers.

Mermaids and manatees do share some surprising similarities. As **mammals**, manatees must occasionally rise to the surface to breathe air. They do so headfirst, just like humans. Their short, paddle-like flippers help manatees swim gracefully. Their flippers could even be mistaken for short human arms. Manatees feed on sea grass in shallow waters. They are likely to be spotted near the shore.

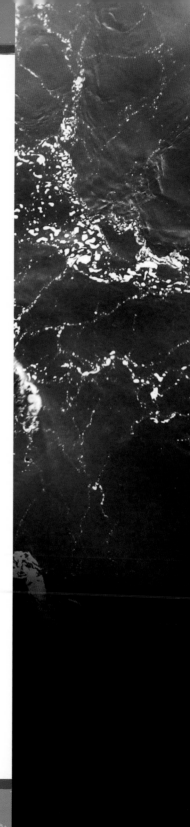

Manatees swim beneath a kayak in Crystal River, Florida.

FACT
Until the mid-1700s, many science book listed mermaids as real creatures. Sailo and explorers had no reason to doubt mermaids existed. They may even have expected to see mermaids. That may explain some earlier sightings.

Manatees are usually peaceful animals.

Other Sea Creatures

Manatees cannot account for all mermaid sightings. Could a whale, dolphin, or porpoise be mistaken for a mermaid? These mammals, called cetaceans, have mermaid-shaped tails. And their four flippers are bony, like human limbs. It is possible that some early mermaids were really whales. But most cetaceans have pointier heads than humans and were probably familiar to early explorers.

Seal Sirens

Imagine being exhausted after a long journey when you hear a sweet song. You look to the nearby shore. You see a creature with a round head, green eyes—and a flipper. Maybe the creature scratches its head.

Is it a mermaid? Scientists say it is probably a seal. Seals like to bask on rocks, where mermaid sightings have often occurred. And unlike silent manatees, seals can utter haunting musical notes. Most seals are gray, but a few are pink or colored like some human skin. They have eyes of every shade. They use flexible flippers to wipe their heads or noses. But there is one problem. Seals are often found lounging on beaches. People likely recognize them as seals before thinking they are mermaids.

A gray seal basks in the sun.

Two seals rest on rocks along the California coast. >

FACT
The ancient Greeks believed in creatures called selkies. This creature was a woman hidden under the skin of a seal.

CHAPTER 3

STUDYING THE EVIDENCE AND THEORIES

Three-quarters of all mermaid sightings occur in waters where no seals or manatees live. How can we explain these other sightings? **Cryptozoology** is the search for animals whose existence has not been proven. Cryptozoologists propose that mermaids are creatures that have not yet been discovered. They point to the discovery of the megamouth shark. This 1,653-pound (750-kilogram), 15-foot- (4.5-m-) long fish was completely unknown until 1976. Members of the U.S. Navy pulled it from the bottom of the sea. Since then, humans have rarely spotted the animal. What other undiscovered creatures could lurk in our waters?

cryptozoology—the study of, and search for, proof of cryptids

Megamouth shark

FACT
The giant panda was once believed to only exist in myth. Today we know the giant panda is a real animal.

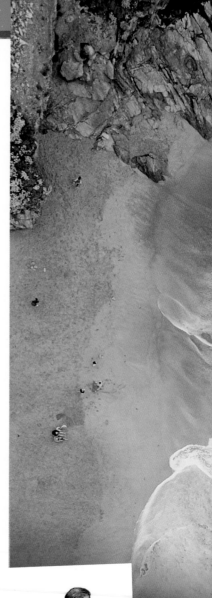

The Missing Link Theory

Could mermaids be our long-lost relatives? Ancient Greek thinker Anaximander believed that all life started in water. He claimed that, as dry land emerged, certain animals learned to live on the land. Over time, they lost their scales and fins.

English naturalist Charles Darwin built on this idea. He proposed his theory of **evolution** in 1859. Some people took this a step further. They thought that if all creatures evolved from sea animals, there might have been a part-human, part-fish creature. This creature could have been a "missing link" between sea creatures and humans. However, in his 1871 book *The Descent of Man*, Darwin suggested that humans descended from relatives of apes, not from sea creatures. Today scientists widely accept Darwin's theory.

Mermaid Hoax

In 1825 villagers of Cornwall, England, were strolling along cliffs overlooking the coast. They heard a haunting melody coming from the shores below. A merman rested on the shore. The creature had the chest of a man and the tail of a fish. It appeared night after night. Years later a man named Robert Hawker admitted it had been a hoax. He had dressed up like a merman. He wanted to show the villagers that it was silly to believe in illogical things.

evolution—the gradual change of living things over long periods of time

fossil—the remains or traces of plants and animals that are preserved as rock

Aquatic Ape Hypothesis

Place one of your hands in front of you, with your knuckles facing up. Spread your hand open as wide as you can. Look at the skin between your fingers. Can you see how it resembles the webbing on the foot of a frog or duck? This is just one reason some scientists have proposed that humans are more closely related to **aquatic** animals than other scientists think. Another reason is that humans are much less hairy than apes. And many hairless mammals, such as elephants and rhinoceroses, have aquatic relatives. One hypothesis says humans came from apes that lived on the shores of lakes. These creatures would have had both aquatic and ape-like features. Perhaps they were the creatures that we call "mermaids."

This is an interesting idea, but when it comes to evidence, this hypothesis doesn't pan out. No "aquatic ape" fossils have ever been found. Humans do have some features in common with aquatic animals. But scientists have other scientifically proven ways to explain these.

aquatic—living or growing in water

An artist's interpretation of how the ancestors of humans may have once lived along waterways

CHAPTER 4
CAN THE MYSTERY BE SOLVED?

Have we solved the mystery of mermaids? Lots of people claim to have spotted mermaids. But many sightings may be cases of mistaken identity with other sea creatures. Others can be explained by hoaxes. Some may be due to wishful thinking or exaggeration. Others are still unexplained. But to prove that mermaids exist, more evidence is needed. So far, no scientific proof for mermaids has been found.

Science cannot prove that mermaids exist. But the investigation has revealed how powerful our desire is to believe. Why do you think humans create hoaxes—or fall for them? Why would we mistake big, bald sea creatures for mermaids? And why would we tell so many stories about mermaids? Mermaids may not exist in reality, but they continue to feed our imaginations.

FACT
In 1822 sea captain Samuel Eades paid $6,000 for a preserved mermaid body. He later discovered it was fake. Someone had wired the body of an orangutan to the tail of a salmon.

SUMMING UP THE SCIENCE

People have proposed all sorts of unusual hypotheses to explain mermaid sightings. Let's see how some of them stand up to science.

Hypothesis	The Science
Mermaids exist, but no solid proof has been found yet.	Until there is proof, we cannot say with certainty that mermaids exist. Since there is no proof, their existence is not likely.
Creatures that closely resembled mermaids once existed but are now extinct or rare. For instance, a species of sea cows that are now extinct might have been mistaken for mermaids.	If true, this hypothesis would only prove the existence of a different type of sea cow, not mermaids. Plus, it would not explain recent mermaid sightings.
Mermaids once existed but are now extinct.	No mermaid fossils have yet been found.

TIMELINE

800s BCE — *The Odyssey* is written, recounting tales of dangerous sirens who lure sailors to ruin.

887 CE — A 195-foot (60-m) "mermaid" is caught off the coast of Scotland. It is probably a whale.

early 1400s — The "Edam mermaid" is discovered in Lake Purmer in the Netherlands.

1493 — Christopher Columbus reports seeing three mermaids jumping out of the water near the coast of Haiti.

1610 — British sea captain Richard Whitbourne reports that a mermaid off the coast of Newfoundland approached him at the shore.

1614 — English sea captain John Smith reports seeing an attractive mermaid near the Caribbean coast.

1700s and 1800s — Fishermen and craftspeople in Japan and the Caribbean create fake mermaids.

1822 — American sea captain Samuel Eades displays the body of a mermaid in London. It is later proved to be a stuffed orangutan and salmon wired together.

1825 — Robert Hawker poses as a merman off the coast of Cornwall, England, fooling nearby villagers.

1967 — Passengers aboard a ferryboat near Vancouver Island, Canada, claim to spot a mermaid. Days later it is revealed to be a hoax.

2004 — After a tsunami hits India, an e-mail claims that a mermaid washed ashore. But the e-mail and photo are discovered to be hoaxes.

2009 — People on the beach near Kiryat Yam, Israel, report regular appearances by a mermaid at sunset.

2013–2014 — Animal Planet airs fake documentaries claiming mermaids exist. Many viewers are fooled into believing the documentaries are based on real science.

GLOSSARY

aquatic (uh-KWAH-tik)—living or growing in water

cryptozoology (kyp-toh-zoo-AHL-uh-jee)—the study of, and search for, proof of cryptids; someone who studies cryptozoology is called a cryptozoologist

evolution (ev-uh-LOO-shuhn)—the gradual change of living things over long periods of time

fossil (FAH-suhl)—the remains or traces of plants and animals that are preserved as rock

hypothesis (hye-POTH-uh-siss)—a prediction that can be tested about how a scientific investigation or experiment will turn out

legend (LEJ-uhnd)—a story handed down from earlier times; legends are often based on fact, but they are not entirely true

mammal (MAM-uhl)—a warm-blooded animal that breathes air; mammals have hair or fur; female mammals feed milk to their young

mythology (mith-AWL-uh-jee)—old or ancient stories told again and again that help connect people with their past

species (SPEE-sheez)—a group of plants or animals that share common characteristics

theory (THEE-ur-ee)—an idea that brings together several hypotheses to explain something

READ MORE

Gerhard, Ken. *A Menagerie of Mysterious Beasts.* Encounters with Cryptid Creatures. Woodbury, Minn.: Llewellyn Publications, 2016.

Light, Kate. *Mermaid Legends.* Famous Legends. New York: Gareth Stevens Publishing, 2018.

Niver, Heather Moore. *Investigating Bigfoot, the Loch Ness Monster, and Other Cryptids.* Understanding the Paranormal. New York: Britannica Educational Publishing, 2016.

INTERNET SITES

Use FactHound to find Internet sites related to this book.

Visit *www.facthound.com*

Just type in 9781543535679 and go.

Check out projects, games and lots more at
www.capstonekids.com

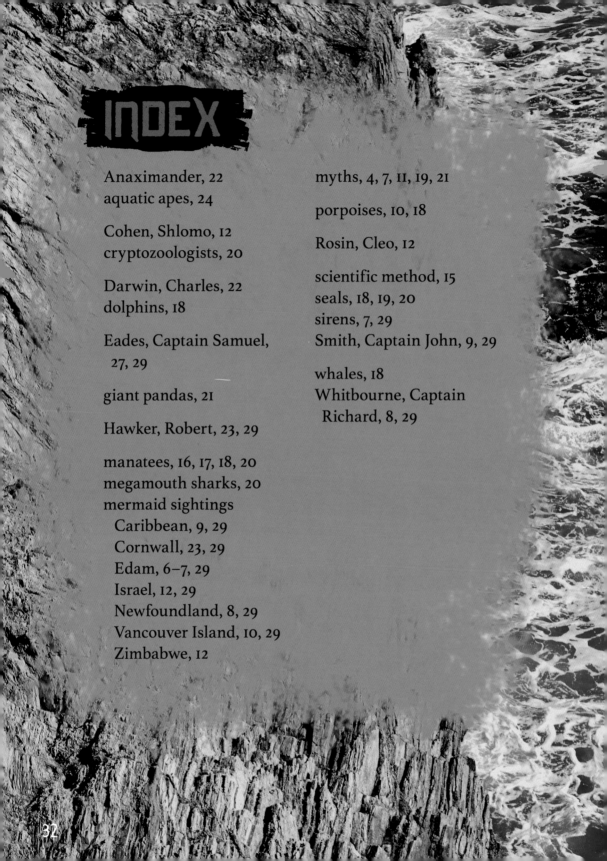

INDEX

Anaximander, 22
aquatic apes, 24

Cohen, Shlomo, 12
cryptozoologists, 20

Darwin, Charles, 22
dolphins, 18

Eades, Captain Samuel,
27, 29

giant pandas, 21

Hawker, Robert, 23, 29

manatees, 16, 17, 18, 20
megamouth sharks, 20
mermaid sightings
    Caribbean, 9, 29
    Cornwall, 23, 29
    Edam, 6–7, 29
    Israel, 12, 29
    Newfoundland, 8, 29
    Vancouver Island, 10, 29
    Zimbabwe, 12

myths, 4, 7, 11, 19, 21

porpoises, 10, 18

Rosin, Cleo, 12

scientific method, 15
seals, 18, 19, 20
sirens, 7, 29
Smith, Captain John, 9, 29

whales, 18
Whitbourne, Captain
    Richard, 8, 29